From Brainstorm to Breakthrough: Techniques and Strategies for Successful Innovation

Frederic BEHE

I. Introduction

Ideation is the process of generating and refining business ideas, and it lies at the heart of entrepreneurship. Successful entrepreneurs are those who can identify unmet needs or gaps in the market, and come up with innovative solutions to address them. However, ideation is not just about generating ideas. It involves understanding the problem, identifying the target market, refining the idea based on feedback, and ultimately bringing it to market.

In this book, we will explore the art and science of ideation. We will provide practical guidance on how to generate and refine business ideas, using a variety of tools and techniques. We will also address common challenges that entrepreneurs face in the ideation process, such as creative blocks, idea overload, and team dynamics. Whether you are an aspiring entrepreneur, an innovation manager in a corporate setting, or simply someone who wants to enhance your creativity and problem-solving skills, this book will provide you with the knowledge and tools you need to succeed.

So, let's get started on the journey of ideation, and discover how you can turn your ideas into successful businesses.

1.1 The importance of ideation in entrepreneurship

Ideation is a critical component of entrepreneurship because it is the starting point of the entrepreneurial journey. Without ideas, there can be no innovation, and without innovation, there can be no entrepreneurship. Ideation is the process of generating and refining business ideas, and it is what separates successful entrepreneurs from those who fail.

Ideation is important for several reasons. Firstly, it allows entrepreneurs to identify unmet needs or gaps in the market. By identifying these gaps, entrepreneurs can create products or services that meet the needs of their target customers. This not only helps to satisfy customer demand, but it also creates new markets and opportunities for growth.

Secondly, ideation allows entrepreneurs to differentiate themselves from competitors. In today's crowded marketplace, it is no longer enough to simply offer a good product or service. Entrepreneurs must find ways to stand out from the crowd, and ideation can help them do that. By creating innovative products or services, entrepreneurs can attract customers and build a loyal customer base.

Thirdly, ideation can help entrepreneurs to create value. By identifying unmet needs or gaps in the market, entrepreneurs can create products or services that provide value to their customers. This can take the form of cost savings, increased efficiency, improved quality, or enhanced convenience. By creating value for customers, entrepreneurs can build a strong brand reputation and increase their chances of long-term success.

In summary, ideation is critical to the success of entrepreneurship because it enables entrepreneurs to identify unmet needs or gaps in the market, differentiate themselves from competitors, and create value for customers. Without ideation, entrepreneurs would be unable to innovate and create the new products and services that are essential for growth and success in today's business landscape.

1.2 Understanding the ideation process

The ideation process is the series of steps that entrepreneurs take to generate and refine business ideas. Understanding the ideation process is critical to successful entrepreneurship because it enables entrepreneurs to systematically generate and evaluate ideas, and ultimately select the most promising ones to pursue.

The ideation process typically involves the following steps:

Understanding the problem:

The first step in the ideation process is to understand the problem that the entrepreneur is trying to solve. This involves identifying unmet needs or gaps in the market, and understanding the pain points of the target customer. By understanding the problem, entrepreneurs can generate ideas that are relevant and useful.

Divergent thinking techniques:

Once the problem has been identified, entrepreneurs can begin to generate ideas. Divergent thinking techniques, such as brainstorming, mind mapping, or SCAMPER, can help entrepreneurs generate a large number of ideas in a short period of time. These techniques encourage the free flow of ideas, without judgment or criticism.

Convergent thinking techniques:

After generating a large number of ideas, entrepreneurs can use convergent thinking techniques, such as SWOT analysis, decision matrices, or the six thinking hats, to evaluate and refine the ideas. These techniques help entrepreneurs to evaluate the feasibility, profitability, and desirability of each idea, and to select the most promising ones to pursue.

Evaluating and selecting ideas:

Once the ideas have been evaluated, entrepreneurs can select the most promising ones to pursue. This involves considering factors such as market potential, competitive landscape, resource availability, and risk.

Refining the idea based on feedback:

Entrepreneurs can refine the selected ideas based on feedback from stakeholders, such as customers, partners, or investors. This helps to ensure that the idea meets the needs of the target customer and has the best chance of success in the marketplace.

The ideation process is a series of steps that entrepreneurs take to generate and refine business ideas. By understanding the process, entrepreneurs can systematically generate and evaluate ideas, and select the most promising ones to pursue. This increases the chances of success and enables entrepreneurs to create innovative products or services that meet the needs of their customers.

II. Generating Ideas

Generating ideas is the first step in the ideation process, and it is critical to the success of entrepreneurship. However, coming up with innovative and viable business ideas is not always easy. It requires creativity, curiosity, and the ability to think outside the box. In this chapter, we will explore various techniques and strategies for generating business ideas, and help you unleash your creativity.

We will begin by discussing the importance of problem identification and how to identify unmet needs or gaps in the market. We will then explore different ideation techniques, such as brainstorming, SCAMPER, and mind mapping, that can help you generate a large number of ideas quickly. We will also cover the role of empathy in ideation, and how to put yourself in the shoes of your target customer to generate customer-centric ideas.

By the end of this chapter, you will have a deeper understanding of the ideation process and the tools and techniques that you can use to generate innovative and viable business ideas. So, let's get started and unleash your creativity!

2.1 Understanding the problem

Before you can generate business ideas, you need to understand the problem you are trying to solve. This means identifying unmet needs or gaps in the market, and understanding the pain points of your target customer.

One way to identify problems is to look at your own experiences and frustrations as a consumer. What products or services do you wish existed that don't? What issues or challenges do you face in your daily life that you think could be solved by a new product or service?

Another way to identify problems is to conduct market research. This can involve analyzing industry trends and data, surveying potential customers, or conducting focus groups. By gathering feedback from your target audience, you can gain insights into their pain points and unmet needs.

Once you have identified a problem, it's important to define it clearly and specifically. This involves breaking it down into its component parts and understanding the underlying causes. For example, if the problem is "lack of healthy food options for busy professionals," you might break it down into sub-problems such as "limited time for meal preparation" and "limited access to healthy food options. »

By breaking down the problem into its component parts, you can begin to brainstorm potential solutions for each sub-problem. This can help you generate a range of ideas that address different aspects of the problem.

Understanding the problem is a critical first step in the ideation process. By identifying unmet needs or gaps in the market, and understanding the pain points of your target customer, you can begin to generate business ideas that address real-world problems. By breaking down the problem into its component parts, you can generate a range of ideas that address different aspects of the problem, and ultimately select the most promising ones to pursue.

2.2 Divergent thinking techniques

Divergent thinking is a creative process that involves generating a large number of ideas in a short amount of time. It is a key component of the ideation process, as it helps you generate a broad range of business ideas quickly. Here are some common divergent thinking techniques:

Brainstorming:

Brainstorming is a classic divergent thinking technique that involves generating as many ideas as possible in a short amount of time, without worrying about their feasibility or quality. The goal is to generate a large quantity of ideas that can later be refined and evaluated.

To conduct a brainstorming session, you should start by defining the problem or challenge you want to address. Then, gather a group of people who have different perspectives and experiences. It can be helpful to have a facilitator to guide the session and keep the group focused.

During the brainstorming session, participants should be encouraged to share their ideas without judgment or criticism. All ideas, no matter how unconventional or unrealistic, should be welcome. Participants can build on each other's ideas and suggest new directions or variations.

One common technique to encourage idea generation is to use prompts or stimuli. These can be words, images, or questions that stimulate creative thinking and help participants generate new ideas. For example, you might use a prompt such as "What if money and time were not an issue?" or "How might we solve this problem using only existing resources? »

It can also be helpful to set a time limit for the brainstorming session. This helps keep the group focused and encourages participants to generate ideas quickly. After the brainstorming session is over, you can evaluate the ideas and select the most promising ones to pursue further.

While brainstorming is a powerful technique for generating a large quantity of ideas quickly, it's important to note that not all ideas are created equal. Some may be impractical, irrelevant, or unfeasible. That's why it's important to evaluate the ideas and select the most promising ones to pursue further. This can involve further research, prototyping, or testing to determine whether the idea is viable and worth pursuing as a business venture.

SCAMPER:

SCAMPER is a structured brainstorming technique that helps you generate new ideas by modifying or adapting existing ones. The acronym stands for:

- Substitute: What can you substitute in the product, service, or process? What if you replace a component or material with something else?

- Combine: What elements can you combine or merge to create something new? What if you combine two or more products or services into one?
- Adapt: What if you adapt the idea to a new context or audience? Can you modify the product or service to better fit the needs of a different market segment?
- Modify: What if you change the product or service in some way? Can you alter its size, shape, or color? Can you add or remove features?
- Put to another use: What other uses could the product or service have? Can it be used in a different industry or market? Can it solve a different problem?
- Eliminate: What if you eliminate a feature or component from the product or service? What if you simplify the process or remove a step?
- Reverse: What if you do the opposite of what's currently being done? What if you turn the product or service upside down or inside out?

To use the SCAMPER technique, you start by selecting an existing product, service, or process and applying each of the seven SCAMPER techniques to it, one at a time. For each technique, you generate as many new ideas as possible before moving on to the next one. The goal is to generate a large number of new ideas that can be evaluated later to determine which ones are worth pursuing further.

For example, let's say you want to generate new ideas for a coffee shop. Here are some potential SCAMPER ideas:

- Substitute: Use almond milk instead of cow's milk. Replace the coffee cups with reusable mugs.
- Combine: Combine coffee with breakfast sandwiches. Create a coffee and dessert pairing menu.
- Adapt: Create a "coffee flight" experience for customers to try different types of coffee. Offer special coffee blends or roasts for different seasons.
- Modify: Offer a "build your own" coffee drink menu. Add seasonal flavors to the menu.
- Put to another use: Host coffee tastings or educational events. Use coffee grounds as compost for a community garden.
- Eliminate: Remove disposable straws and stirrers. Simplify the ordering process by using a self-serve kiosk.

- Reverse: Create a coffee shop that only serves decaf coffee. Create a coffee shop where customers can bring their own coffee beans to be brewed.

By using the SCAMPER technique, you can generate a large number of new ideas and variations quickly, without starting from scratch. The technique encourages you to think creatively and consider alternative approaches to existing products, services, or processes.

Mind Mapping: Mind Mapping:

Mind mapping is a visual brainstorming technique that involves creating a diagram to visually organize information around a central concept or theme. It's a great way to generate new ideas and explore different possibilities by connecting and expanding upon related ideas.
To create a mind map, start by writing the central concept or theme in the center of a blank sheet of paper or digital document. From there, branch out and add related ideas, subtopics, and details around the central concept, connecting them with lines or arrows. You can continue to expand and connect the ideas until you've exhausted all possibilities.
Mind mapping allows you to see the connections and relationships between different ideas, which can help you generate new ideas or refine existing ones. It also encourages non-linear thinking, which can help you break free from traditional patterns of thought and discover new perspectives.
For example, let's say you want to generate new ideas for a social media marketing campaign. Here's a potential mind map:

Central concept: Social media marketing campaign

Subtopics:

- Target audience
- Platform selection
- Content ideas
- Budget
- Timeline

Target audience:

- Demographics
- Interests
- Pain points
- Behaviors

Platform selection:

- Facebook
- Instagram
- Twitter
- LinkedIn
- TikTok

Content ideas:

- Visuals (photos, videos, graphics)
- User-generated content
- Hashtag campaigns
- Influencer partnerships

Budget:

- Paid advertising
- Boosting posts
- Sponsored content
- Giveaways

Timeline:

- Launch date
- Post frequency
- Campaign duration
- Metrics tracking

By using the mind mapping technique, you can visually organize your ideas and explore different possibilities for your social media marketing campaign. You can also identify any gaps or areas that need further development. The technique can be applied to any brainstorming situation and can be done individually or as a group activity.

Random Word Association:

Random word association is a technique that involves generating new ideas by making connections between seemingly unrelated words. The process is simple: start with a random word and then brainstorm as many ideas as possible that connect that word to your business idea or problem.

To use this technique, start by selecting a random word. This word can be generated using a tool such as a word generator or simply by selecting a word at random from a dictionary or book. Then, brainstorm as many ideas as possible that connect the random word to your business idea or problem. The ideas don't have to be logical or practical at first, as the goal is to generate as many possibilities as possible. Once you have a list of ideas, you can refine and develop the most promising ones.

Random word association can help you break free from traditional patterns of thought and generate new and unexpected ideas. By connecting seemingly unrelated words, you can discover new perspectives and approaches to your business idea or problem.

Let's say you're trying to generate new ideas for a mobile app that helps people manage their finances. Here's a potential random word association:

Random word: Tree

Ideas:

- A tree-themed app that helps people plant and grow their savings
- A feature that shows users the impact of their financial decisions on the environment
- An app that tracks and analyzes the spending habits of people who live in treehouses

- A tree-based currency that rewards users for saving money
- A social network for people who share an interest in sustainable living and personal finance

By using the random word association technique, you can come up with unique and unexpected ideas for your mobile app that you might not have thought of otherwise.

Role-playing:

Role-playing is a technique that involves acting out different scenarios or perspectives to generate new ideas. This technique is particularly useful when you're trying to understand a customer's perspective or develop a new product or service.

To use this technique, start by identifying the scenario or perspective you want to explore. This could be a customer experience, a new product idea, or a marketing strategy. Then, assign roles to participants who will act out the scenario. This could include the customer, salesperson, or product developer, for example. Participants can then act out the scenario, taking on the perspectives and behaviors of their assigned roles. This process can help you gain new insights and perspectives on your business idea or problem.

Role-playing can also help you anticipate potential challenges or issues and develop solutions before they arise. By acting out different scenarios, you can identify potential pain points and develop strategies to address them.

Let's say you're developing a new product for a fitness company and want to explore the customer experience.

Here's a potential role-playing scenario:

Scenario:

A customer is interested in purchasing a fitness tracker from the company and has questions about the product.

Roles:

- Customer
- Salesperson

Tho participants would then act out the scenario, with the salesperson providing information and answering the customer's questions. Through this process, you could gain new insights into the customer's perspective and identify potential pain points or areas for improvement.

Role-playing can be done individually or as a group activity and can be adapted to different scenarios and perspectives. It can be particularly useful when trying to understand customer experiences or develop new products or services.

By using these divergent thinking techniques, you can generate a large number of business ideas quickly and efficiently. The goal is to generate as many ideas as possible, without worrying about their feasibility or quality. Later, you can refine and evaluate these ideas to determine which ones are most promising and worth pursuing further.

2.3 Convergent thinking techniques

Convergent thinking is a process of narrowing down ideas and focusing on the best solutions. This type of thinking is useful when you have generated a large number of ideas and need to refine and develop them into practical solutions.

Here are a few techniques you can use to apply convergent thinking to generate and refine business ideas:

SWOT Analysis:

SWOT analysis is a framework for identifying the strengths, weaknesses, opportunities, and threats of a business idea. This technique can help you evaluate the viability and potential success of your idea by considering both internal and external factors.

To conduct a SWOT analysis, you will need to:

- Identify the strengths of your idea: What are the unique advantages and benefits of your idea? What makes it stand out from the competition?
- Identify the weaknesses of your idea: What are the potential drawbacks or limitations of your idea? Are there any factors that could hinder its success?
- Identify the opportunities for your idea: What are the potential markets or customer segments for your idea? Are there any trends or changes in the industry that could create opportunities for your idea?
- Identify the threats to your idea: What are the potential obstacles or challenges that could impact the success of your idea? Are there any competitors or external factors that could pose a threat to your idea?

Once you have identified these factors, you can use them to evaluate the overall viability and potential success of your idea. For example, if your idea has strong strengths and opportunities, but also has significant weaknesses and threats, you may need to refine or pivot your idea to address these challenges.

SWOT analysis can be particularly useful when evaluating new business ideas, developing marketing strategies, or assessing the performance of a current business. By considering both internal and external factors, you can identify potential challenges and opportunities and develop strategies to address them.

For example, let's say you're considering launching a new line of organic skincare products. Here's how you might conduct a SWOT analysis:

Strengths:

- Use of organic and natural ingredients
- Appeal to health-conscious and environmentally conscious customers
- Potential for high profit margins

Weaknesses:

- Limited brand recognition and market share
- High production costs for organic ingredients
- Competition from established skincare brands

Opportunities:

- Growing demand for organic and natural skincare products
- Potential to expand into international markets
- Opportunities for partnerships with eco-friendly retailers and influencers

Threats:

- Intense competition from established skincare brands
- Potential changes in regulations or consumer preferences for organic products
- Fluctuations in the availability and cost of organic ingredients

By conducting a SWOT analysis, you can evaluate the potential strengths, weaknesses, opportunities, and threats of your idea and develop a plan of action to address them.

Prioritization Matrix:

The prioritization matrix is a tool for evaluating and prioritizing ideas based on multiple criteria. This technique can help you compare and prioritize different ideas based on factors such as feasibility, impact, and cost.

To conduct a prioritization matrix, you will need to:

Identify the criteria for evaluation:

What factors are most important for evaluating the success and feasibility of your idea? Examples may include impact, feasibility, cost, time to market, etc.

Assign weights to each criteria:

Assign a weight to each criteria to reflect its relative importance in the overall evaluation process. For example, if impact is more important than cost, assign a higher weight to impact.

Score each idea based on the criteria:

Evaluate each idea based on each criteria and assign a score between 1 and 5 (or any other relevant scale). The higher the score, the better the idea performs in that criteria.

Multiply scores by weights:

Multiply the scores by the weights to calculate a weighted score for each criteria.

Calculate the overall score for each idea:

Add up the weighted scores for each criteria to calculate an overall score for each idea. The higher the overall score, the more promising the idea.

Once you have calculated the overall score for each idea, you can use this information to prioritize and select the most promising ideas for further development.

For example, let's say you're considering three different business ideas for a new startup. Here's how you might conduct a prioritization matrix:

Criteria:

- Impact: 40%
- Feasibility: 30%
- Cost: 20%
- Time to market: 10%
-

Weights:

- Impact: 4
- Feasibility: 3
- Cost: 2
- Time to market: 1

o Idea 1:

- Impact: 5
- Feasibility: 3
- Cost: 2
- Time to market: 4

Weighted scores:

- Impact: 20 (5 x 4)
- Feasibility: 9 (3 x 3)
- Cost: 4 (2 x 2)
- Time to market: 4 (1 x 4

Overall score: 37 (20 + 9 + 4 + 4)

o Idea 2:

- Impact: 4
- Feasibility: 4
- Cost: 3
- Time to market: 3

Weighted scores:

- Impact: 16 (4 x 4)
- Feasibility: 12 (4 x 3)
- Cost: 6 (3 x 2)
- Time to market: 3 (1 x 3)

Overall score: 37 (16 + 12 + 6 + 3)

○ Idea 3:

- Impact: 3
- Feasibility: 5
- Cost: 4
- Time to market: 5

Weighted scores:

- Impact: 12 (3 x 4)
- Feasibility: 15 (5 x 3)
- Cost: 8 (4 x 2)
- Time to market: 5 (1 x 5)

Overall score: 40 (12 + 15 + 8 + 5)

Based on this prioritization matrix, Idea 3 appears to be the most promising, with the highest overall score. You can use this information to prioritize and focus on developing Idea 3 further, while potentially revising or discarding the other two ideas.

The prioritization matrix is a valuable tool for evaluating and prioritizing ideas based on multiple criteria. By considering a range

Cost-Benefit Analysis:

Cost-Benefit Analysis (CBA) is a technique used to compare the costs of a particular course of action to its benefits. This method is commonly used in business decision-making processes, as it allows decision-makers to weigh the potential costs and benefits of different options before making a final decision.

The first step in conducting a CBA is to identify all the costs and benefits associated with each option. These can include both monetary and non-monetary factors. For example, the cost of investing in new equipment or hiring additional staff would be a monetary cost, while the potential increase in revenue resulting from the investment would be a benefit. Non-monetary factors could include intangible benefits such as improved customer satisfaction or increased employee morale.

Once all costs and benefits have been identified, they are quantified in monetary terms. This allows decision-makers to compare the financial impact of each option. To do this, the costs and benefits are converted into present value terms using a discount rate. The discount rate represents the opportunity cost of investing money in one option versus another, and is typically based on the cost of capital or the rate of return on alternative investments.

The final step in a CBA is to compare the total costs and benefits of each option. If the benefits outweigh the costs, the option is deemed to be financially viable and may be pursued. If the costs outweigh the benefits, the option is deemed to be too costly and is typically rejected.

CBA is a powerful tool for decision-making, but it does have some limitations. For example, it assumes that all costs and benefits can be quantified in monetary terms, which may not always be the case. Additionally, the discount rate used can have a significant impact on the results of the analysis, and may be subject to debate or uncertainty. Nevertheless, CBA remains a popular and effective technique for evaluating the financial viability of different options.

Risk Assessment:

Risk assessment is a process used to identify, evaluate, and prioritize potential risks associated with a particular course of action. This technique is commonly used in business decision-making processes, as it allows decision-makers to identify potential risks and take steps to mitigate them before making a final decision.

The first step in conducting a risk assessment is to identify potential risks associated with each option. These risks can include a wide range of factors, such as economic, political, regulatory, and environmental risks. Once risks have been identified, they are evaluated in terms of their likelihood and potential impact. This helps to prioritize risks and focus mitigation efforts on the most significant risks.

The second step in a risk assessment is to develop a plan to mitigate identified risks. This can include a range of strategies, such as hedging against economic risks, lobbying for favorable regulatory changes, or investing in environmental sustainability measures. The specific mitigation strategies used will depend on the nature of the risks identified, as well as the resources and capabilities of the organization involved.

The final step in a risk assessment is to monitor and evaluate the effectiveness of the mitigation strategies implemented. This helps decision-makers to identify any new risks that may arise, and to adjust mitigation strategies as needed to ensure continued risk management.

Risk assessment is a powerful tool for decision-making, but it does have some limitations. For example, it relies on assumptions and estimates, which may be subject to error or uncertainty. Additionally, it can be difficult to quantify the potential impact of some risks, particularly those related to non-financial factors such as reputation or brand image. Nevertheless, risk assessment remains a valuable technique for identifying and mitigating potential risks associated with different options.

By applying convergent thinking techniques to your business ideas, you can identify the best solutions and refine them into practical plans for implementation. These techniques can help you evaluate and prioritize your ideas, as well as identify potential risks and challenges.

Let's say you have generated a large number of ideas for a new product line for your company. Here's how you might use a convergent thinking technique like SWOT analysis:

- List out the strengths, weaknesses, opportunities, and threats of each idea.
- Evaluate how each factor impacts the viability and success of the idea.
- Use this information to narrow down the list of ideas to the most promising ones.
- Refine and develop these ideas into practical plans for implementation.

By using convergent thinking techniques like SWOT analysis, you can identify the best solutions and develop a plan of action for implementing them.

2.4 Evaluating and selecting ideas

After generating a list of potential business ideas using the divergent and convergent thinking techniques outlined in the previous chapters, it is important to evaluate and select the most promising ideas to move forward with. The goal of this process is to identify the ideas that have the greatest potential for success and align with the overall goals and values of the organization.

The evaluation and selection process typically involves the following steps:

1. **Defining evaluation criteria:**

It is important to define clear and measurable criteria for evaluating the potential of each idea. This can include factors such as market size, profitability, competitive landscape, feasibility, and strategic fit.

2. **Scoring and ranking ideas:**

Once the evaluation criteria have been defined, each idea can be scored and ranked based on how well they meet these criteria. This can be done using a variety of methods, such as a scoring matrix or a decision-making tree.

3. **Narrowing down the list:**

After scoring and ranking each idea, the list can be narrowed down to the top few ideas that meet the evaluation criteria and have the greatest potential for success.

4. **Conducting feasibility studies:**

Once the list has been narrowed down, feasibility studies can be conducted to assess the practicality and viability of each idea. This can include market research, financial analysis, and operational planning.

5. **Selecting the best idea:**

After conducting feasibility studies, the best idea can be selected based on its potential for success, alignment with organizational goals and values, and practicality and feasibility.

It is important to note that the evaluation and selection process is not a one-time event, but an ongoing process that should be revisited regularly as new information becomes available. Additionally, it is important to involve key stakeholders in the evaluation and selection process to ensure buy-in and support for the chosen idea.

III. Refining Ideas

After generating and evaluating a list of potential business ideas, the next step in the ideation process is to refine and develop the most promising ideas. The goal of this phase is to take the initial idea and develop it into a viable and sustainable business concept.

Refining ideas involves a process of iteration and experimentation, where ideas are tested and refined based on feedback and new information. This process typically involves the following steps:

Clarifying the idea:

The first step in refining an idea is to clarify and define it in more detail. This can include developing a clear value proposition, identifying target customers, and defining the product or service offering.

Conducting market research:

Once the idea has been clarified, it is important to conduct market research to validate the idea and assess the competitive landscape. This can include analyzing industry trends, identifying customer needs and preferences, and assessing the strengths and weaknesses of competitors.

Testing the concept:

After conducting market research, the next step is to test the concept in the marketplace. This can include creating a minimum viable product (MVP) and testing it with a select group of customers to gather feedback and refine the idea.

Refining the business model:

Based on feedback and market research, the business model can be refined and optimized to better meet customer needs and achieve profitability. This can involve adjusting the pricing strategy, refining the marketing approach, or exploring new revenue streams.

Scaling the business:

Once the concept has been refined and validated, the final step is to scale the business and bring the product or service to market. This can involve developing a go-to-market strategy, building a team, and securing funding to support growth and expansion.

The process of refining ideas is crucial to the success of any new business venture. By taking the time to clarify and validate the initial idea, test it in the marketplace, and refine the business model, entrepreneurs can increase the likelihood of success and build a sustainable and thriving business.

3.1 Defining the target market

Defining the target market is a critical step in the process of refining business ideas. The target market refers to the specific group of customers that a product or service is designed to serve. Understanding the needs, preferences, and behaviors of the target market is essential for developing a product or service that meets their needs and stands out from competitors.

To define the target market, entrepreneurs can start by conducting market research to gather data on the demographics, psychographics, and buying behaviors of potential customers. This can include analyzing census data, conducting surveys, or using focus groups to gather feedback and insights.

Once data has been gathered, entrepreneurs can use it to create customer profiles, also known as buyer personas. These profiles describe the characteristics and behaviors of the ideal customer, including age, gender, income, education level, buying habits, and values.

Defining the target market can also involve segmenting the market into smaller subgroups based on shared characteristics or needs. This can help entrepreneurs to tailor their marketing and product development efforts to specific segments of the market, and to develop a more targeted and effective marketing strategy.

Defining the target market is essential for developing a successful product or service that meets the needs of a specific group of customers. By understanding the characteristics and behaviors of the target market, entrepreneurs can develop a product or service that is more likely to succeed in the marketplace and achieve long-term growth and profitability.

3.2 Identifying the unique value proposition

Identifying the unique value proposition is a critical step in refining business ideas. A value proposition is a statement that explains the unique benefit that a product or service provides to customers. It describes the key features and benefits of the product or service, as well as how it solves a specific problem or meets a particular need of the target market.

To identify the unique value proposition, entrepreneurs need to start by conducting a thorough analysis of their product or service, as well as their competitors. They should consider factors such as pricing, quality, features, and benefits, as well as any potential gaps in the market that their product or service could fill.

Entrepreneurs can use a variety of tools and techniques to help them identify their unique value proposition. For example, they can conduct a SWOT analysis to assess their strengths, weaknesses, opportunities, and threats, and to identify areas where they can differentiate themselves from their competitors.

Another useful technique is to conduct a customer needs analysis, which involves gathering feedback and insights from potential customers to understand their needs, pain points, and preferences. This can help entrepreneurs to identify the features and benefits that are most important to their target market, and to develop a unique value proposition that addresses those needs.

The unique value proposition should be clear, concise, and compelling. It should clearly communicate the benefits of the product or service, and explain why it is the best choice for customers in the target market. By identifying and articulating a strong unique value proposition, entrepreneurs can differentiate themselves from their competitors and increase the likelihood of success in the marketplace.

3.3 Conducting market research

Conducting market research is an essential step in refining business ideas. It involves gathering information about the target market, competitors, industry trends, and other factors that can impact the success of the business.

There are several different methods that entrepreneurs can use to conduct market research, depending on their specific needs and goals.

Some common methods include:

Surveys:

Surveys are one of the most common methods of conducting market research. They involve gathering information from a sample of potential customers about their needs, preferences, and behaviors.

Surveys can be conducted through a variety of methods, including online, by phone, or in person. Online surveys are often the most convenient and cost-effective option, as they can be distributed widely and easily analyzed using online survey tools.

When designing a survey, it's important to consider the specific information that needs to be gathered and the target audience. This will help to ensure that the survey is effective in gathering meaningful data.

Some tips for designing effective surveys include:

Keep it short and focused:

Long surveys can be overwhelming for respondents and can result in lower response rates. Focus on gathering the most important information and keep the survey as short as possible.

Use clear and concise language:

Use language that is easy to understand and avoid jargon or technical terms that may be unfamiliar to respondents.

Offer incentives:

Offering an incentive, such as a discount or gift card, can increase response rates and encourage respondents to provide thoughtful answers. Test the survey: Before launching the survey, test it with a small group of respondents to identify any potential issues or areas for improvement.

Once the survey has been completed, the data can be analyzed to identify key trends and insights. This information can then be used to refine the business idea and develop a marketing strategy that is tailored to the needs and preferences of the target market.

Surveys can be a valuable tool for entrepreneurs looking to gather information about their target market and refine their business ideas. By following best practices for survey design and analysis, entrepreneurs can gather meaningful data that can inform their decision-making and increase the likelihood of success in the marketplace.

Focus groups:

Focus groups are another popular method of conducting market research. They involve gathering a small group of individuals who are representative of the target market and facilitating a discussion about their needs, preferences, and opinions related to a particular product or service.

Focus groups can be conducted in person or online, and typically last for 60-90 minutes. They are typically led by a facilitator who guides the discussion and asks open-ended questions to encourage participants to share their thoughts and ideas.

Some advantages of focus groups include:

- In-depth insights: Focus groups allow for more in-depth insights into the attitudes and opinions of potential customers. Participants are able to share their thoughts and ideas in a group setting, which can lead to more robust and diverse feedback.
- Interactive discussion: Focus groups allow for interactive discussion between participants, which can lead to new ideas and insights that may not have been uncovered through other research methods.
- Real-time feedback: Focus groups provide real-time feedback that can be used to refine the business idea or marketing strategy.

However, there are also some limitations to consider when using focus groups.
For example:

- Small sample size: Focus groups typically involve a small sample size, which may not be representative of the broader target market.
- Group dynamics: The dynamics of the group can impact the feedback that is provided. For example, some participants may dominate the discussion while others may be hesitant to share their thoughts.
- Potential for bias: Participants may be influenced by the opinions of others in the group, which can impact the accuracy of the feedback provided.

Overall, focus groups can be a valuable tool for entrepreneurs looking to gather insights into the attitudes and opinions of their target market. By following best practices for focus group design and analysis, entrepreneurs can gather meaningful data that can inform their decision-making and increase the likelihood of success in the marketplace.

Interviews:

Interviews are a common method of conducting market research in which an entrepreneur directly asks potential customers or other stakeholders a series of open-ended questions to gather information about their needs, preferences, and opinions related to a particular product or service.

There are several different types of interviews that entrepreneurs can conduct, including:

- Structured interviews: These interviews involve asking a standardized set of questions to all participants in the same order. This approach is useful for gathering consistent data that can be easily compared across participants.
- Semi-structured interviews: These interviews involve asking a set of open-ended questions but allowing the conversation to flow more naturally. This approach is useful for gathering detailed, qualitative data that can provide deeper insights into participants' thoughts and opinions.
- Unstructured interviews: These interviews involve having a more casual conversation with participants and allowing them to lead the discussion. This approach is useful for gathering unexpected insights and ideas that may not have been uncovered through other research methods.

Some advantages of interviews include:

- In-depth insights: Interviews allow for more in-depth insights into the attitudes and opinions of potential customers. Participants are able to share their thoughts and ideas in a one-on-one setting, which can lead to more detailed and personal feedback.
- Flexibility: Interviews can be conducted in person, over the phone, or online, which allows entrepreneurs to gather feedback from a wide range of participants.
- Ability to clarify responses: In an interview, the entrepreneur can ask follow-up questions or clarify responses in real-time, which can lead to more accurate and meaningful data.

There are also some limitations to consider when using interviews. For example:

- Small sample size: Interviews typically involve a small sample size, which may not be representative of the broader target market.
- Potential for bias: Participants may not be fully honest or may provide socially desirable responses, which can impact the accuracy of the feedback provided.
- Time-consuming: Conducting interviews can be time-consuming and resource-intensive, particularly if the entrepreneur is conducting many interviews.

Interviews can be a valuable tool for entrepreneurs looking to gather insights into the attitudes and opinions of their target market. By following best practices for interview design and analysis, entrepreneurs can gather meaningful data that can inform their decision-making and increase the likelihood of success in the marketplace.

Secondary research:

Secondary research is a research method that involves analyzing and synthesizing information that has already been collected by other sources. This can include data from published reports, academic studies, industry publications, and government sources, among others.

Some advantages of secondary research include:

- Cost-effective: Secondary research is often less expensive than primary research methods, such as surveys or focus groups, as the data has already been collected.
- Time-efficient: Secondary research can be conducted quickly as the data is readily available.
- Provides context: Secondary research can provide a broader context for understanding the industry, market trends, and consumer behavior.

There are also some limitations to consider when using secondary research. For example:

- Quality of data: The quality of secondary data can vary widely and may not be as reliable as primary data. It's important to evaluate the credibility and relevance of the sources being used.
- Limited control: Researchers have limited control over the data that is available through secondary sources and may not be able to access certain information.
- Lack of customization: Secondary data is not tailored to the specific needs of the researcher and may not provide all the information necessary for decision-making.

Secondary research can be a valuable tool for entrepreneurs looking to gather information about their target market and industry trends. By carefully selecting and evaluating sources, entrepreneurs can gain insights into consumer behavior and market dynamics that can inform their decision-making and increase the likelihood of success in the marketplace.

By conducting market research, entrepreneurs can gain a better understanding of their target market, identify opportunities and challenges, and refine their business ideas based on customer needs and preferences. It can also help them to identify potential competitors and develop strategies for differentiating themselves in the marketplace. Ultimately, conducting thorough market research is critical for developing a successful business plan and increasing the likelihood of success in the marketplace.

3.4 Refining the idea based on feedback

Refining the idea based on feedback is an essential step in the ideation process. It involves gathering feedback from potential customers, stakeholders, and experts in the field to gain insights into how the idea can be improved or modified to better meet the needs of the market.

There are several methods for gathering feedback, including:

Customer feedback surveys:

Surveys can be a useful tool for gathering feedback from potential customers. Questions can be tailored to gather specific information about the product or service, such as pricing, features, and overall appeal.

User testing:

User testing involves having potential customers try out a prototype or early version of the product or service and provide feedback on their experience. This can provide valuable insights into usability, functionality, and potential areas for improvement.

Expert feedback:

Experts in the field can provide valuable feedback on the feasibility and potential of the idea. This can include feedback on market demand, competition, and potential challenges or opportunities.

Once feedback has been gathered, it's important to carefully consider the information and use it to refine the idea. This may involve making changes to the product or service based on customer feedback, adjusting pricing or marketing strategies based on expert feedback, or rethinking the overall value proposition of the idea.

The goal of refining the idea based on feedback is to create a product or service that better meets the needs of the market and is more likely to be successful in the marketplace. By gathering and using feedback effectively, entrepreneurs can increase the chances of success and reduce the risk of failure.

IV. Ideation in Action

Ideation in Action is the fourth section of the book, which focuses on the practical application of ideation concepts and techniques. In this section, we will explore case studies and real-world examples of successful ideation in action, as well as provide practical advice for entrepreneurs looking to implement ideation strategies in their own businesses.

This section is designed to help readers move beyond theory and into practice, by showcasing real-world examples of ideation success stories and providing actionable advice on how to implement ideation techniques in a business context. Whether you are an aspiring entrepreneur looking to launch a new business, or an established business owner seeking to innovate and grow, the strategies and case studies presented in this section can help you achieve your goals.

Topics covered in this section include:

- The ideation process in action: Case studies of successful ideation processes used by real companies to generate and refine business ideas.
- Ideation tools and techniques: A practical guide to using the ideation techniques discussed in earlier sections, such as brainstorming, mind mapping, and SWOT analysis, in a real-world context.
- Implementing ideation strategies: Practical advice on how to integrate ideation strategies into your business, including tips on team collaboration, project management, and measuring success.

By exploring real-world examples and providing practical advice, Ideation in Action aims to empower entrepreneurs and business leaders to generate and refine successful business ideas using proven ideation techniques and strategies.

4.1 Creating a business model canvas

Creating a business model canvas is a vital step in the ideation process, as it helps entrepreneurs to visualize and communicate their business idea in a clear and concise way. The business model canvas is a tool that helps entrepreneurs to articulate the key elements of their business model, including the value proposition, customer segments, channels, revenue streams, cost structure, and key partners and resources.

The business model canvas is structured around nine key components, each of which is essential to the success of the business.

These components are:

- Customer segments: Identifying the target customers and their specific needs and preferences.

- Value proposition: Defining the unique value that the business offers to its customers.

- Channels: Identifying the channels through which the business will reach its customers.

- Customer relationships: Describing the types of relationships the business will have with its customers.

- Revenue streams: Identifying the sources of revenue for the business.

- Key activities: Identifying the key activities that the business must undertake to deliver its value proposition.

- Key resources: Identifying the key resources (e.g. people, technology, assets) needed to deliver the value proposition.

- Key partners: Identifying the key partners (e.g. suppliers, distributors, service providers) needed to deliver the value proposition.

- Cost structure: Identifying the costs associated with delivering the value proposition.

Creating a business model canvas requires careful consideration of each of these components, and how they fit together to form a coherent business model. The canvas can be used to communicate the business idea to stakeholders, and to identify potential strengths, weaknesses, and areas for improvement in the business model.

The business model canvas is a flexible tool that can be adapted to different types of businesses and industries, and can be used at any stage of the ideation process, from initial idea generation to refining and scaling an existing business.

4.2 Prototyping and testing

Prototyping and testing are critical steps in the ideation process, as they enable entrepreneurs to test and refine their business ideas in a low-risk environment before investing significant time and resources into full-scale development.

Prototyping involves creating a preliminary version of the product or service, which can be used to test its functionality, usability, and appeal to customers. Prototypes can take many forms, from physical mockups to digital simulations, and can be used to test different aspects of the product or service, such as its design, features, or pricing.

Testing involves gathering feedback from potential customers, stakeholders, and other relevant parties on the prototype, and using this feedback to refine the idea. Testing can take many forms, such as surveys, focus groups, or user testing, and can provide valuable insights into how the product or service is perceived and how it can be improved.

Prototyping and testing can help entrepreneurs to:

- Validate the business idea: By testing the product or service with potential customers, entrepreneurs can gain valuable feedback on whether the idea is viable and whether it meets the needs and preferences of the target market.

- Identify areas for improvement: By gathering feedback on the prototype, entrepreneurs can identify areas where the product or service can be improved, such as its design, features, or pricing.

- Refine the business model: By testing different aspects of the business model, such as revenue streams or customer segments, entrepreneurs can refine their approach and identify potential areas for growth and profitability.

- Reduce risk: By testing the business idea in a low-risk environment, entrepreneurs can avoid investing significant time and resources into a product or service that may not be successful in the market.

Prototyping and testing are essential steps in the ideation process, as they enable entrepreneurs to validate and refine their business ideas, and to increase the chances of success when launching a new product or service.

4.3 Pitching the idea to investors

 pitching an idea to investors is a crucial step in turning an idea into a successful business. A pitch is essentially a presentation to persuade investors to invest in the idea or business. It is important to prepare a pitch that is concise, clear, and compelling.

To begin, it is important to understand the audience and what they are looking for. Investors are typically looking for ideas that have a strong potential for growth and profitability. Therefore, it is important to focus on the key benefits of the idea and how it will generate revenue.

The pitch should begin with an attention-grabbing introduction that provides a clear overview of the idea and its unique value proposition. This should be followed by a detailed explanation of the product or service, including its features, benefits, and target market. It is important to demonstrate a thorough understanding of the market and competitors, as well as any potential challenges or risks.

In addition to the content of the pitch, the delivery is also important. The presenter should be confident and passionate about the idea, while also being able to respond to questions and concerns from the investors. Visual aids such as slides or a prototype can also be useful in demonstrating the idea.

The goal of the pitch is to persuade the investors to invest in the idea or business. Therefore, it is important to end the pitch with a clear call to action, such as a request for funding or a follow-up meeting.

4.4 Launching and scaling the business

Launching and scaling a business can be challenging but is an exciting step in turning an idea into a successful venture.

The following are some key steps to consider when launching and scaling a business:

1. Develop a solid business plan:

A business plan outlines the strategy, goals, and objectives of the business. It should include a detailed analysis of the target market, competitors, and financial projections.

2. Secure funding:

Depending on the size and complexity of the business, funding may be required to launch and scale the business. This can come from a variety of sources such as angel investors, venture capitalists, or loans from financial institutions.

3. Build a team:

As the business grows, it will be important to build a team of talented individuals who can help execute the vision and mission of the company.

4. Establish partnerships and collaborations:

Partnerships and collaborations can help to expand the reach and impact of the business. This can include partnerships with other businesses or organizations, as well as collaborations with suppliers or vendors.

5. Develop a marketing strategy:

A marketing strategy will help to promote the business and generate interest and awareness among potential customers. This can include a mix of digital and traditional marketing techniques, as well as social media and content marketing.

6. **Monitor and evaluate performance:**

As the business scales, it is important to monitor and evaluate performance regularly. This can include tracking key performance indicators (KPIs) such as revenue, profit margin, and customer acquisition and retention rates.

7. **Pivot and adapt:**

As the business evolves, it may be necessary to pivot or adapt the strategy to respond to changing market conditions or customer needs.

Launching and scaling a business requires a strong commitment, hard work, and a willingness to learn and adapt. By following these key steps, entrepreneurs can turn their ideas into successful and sustainable businesses.

V. Overcoming Common Challenges in Ideation

In this section, we will discuss some of the common challenges that entrepreneurs face during the ideation process and how to overcome them. Developing and refining business ideas can be a challenging process, and it's common to encounter roadblocks and obstacles along the way. In this section, we will explore how to overcome challenges such as idea overload, lack of inspiration, and difficulty in prioritizing ideas. By addressing these challenges, entrepreneurs can move forward with confidence in their chosen ideas and take the necessary steps to bring their business to life.

5.1 Overcoming creative blocks

Creative blocks can be one of the most significant challenges during the ideation process. Sometimes, even the most creative and innovative entrepreneurs can get stuck and struggle to come up with new ideas.

Here are some tips for overcoming creative blocks:

Take a break:

Taking a break is a simple but effective way to overcome creative blocks. Sometimes, the pressure of coming up with ideas can lead to mental fatigue, making it difficult to think creatively. In such cases, taking a break can help to refresh the mind and get the creative juices flowing again.

A break can involve stepping away from the task at hand for a few minutes or engaging in a different activity altogether. This could include going for a walk, listening to music, practicing mindfulness, or engaging in a hobby. By giving the mind a chance to rest and refocus, individuals can often return to the task with renewed energy and fresh perspectives.

Research has shown that taking breaks can have a positive impact on productivity and creativity. In fact, studies have found that individuals who take regular breaks are often more productive and efficient than those who try to power through without taking any breaks.

Taking a break is a simple yet effective strategy for overcoming creative blocks and maintaining productivity and creativity.

Change your environment:

Changing your environment is another way to overcome creative blocks. Sometimes, being in the same environment for an extended period can lead to mental fatigue and reduce creativity. In such cases, changing the environment can help to stimulate the mind and spark new ideas.

Changing the environment can involve anything from working in a different room or location to taking a trip to a new city or country. By exposing yourself to new surroundings, you can tap into new experiences and perspectives, which can inspire fresh ideas and solutions.

Research has shown that environmental factors such as lighting, colors, and sounds can have a significant impact on creativity. For example, studies have found that natural light and greenery can increase productivity and creativity.

Changing your environment is a simple yet effective strategy for overcoming creative blocks and increasing creativity. By exposing yourself to new surroundings and environmental factors, you can stimulate your mind and unlock new ideas and solutions.

Collaborate with others:

Collaborating with others is another effective way to overcome creative blocks. Sometimes, working alone can limit your perspective and ideas, leading to mental blocks. Collaborating with others can bring fresh ideas and perspectives, which can stimulate creativity and spark new ideas.

Collaboration can involve working with colleagues, peers, or experts in a particular field. By working together, you can share knowledge and experiences, brainstorm ideas, and challenge each other's thinking, leading to more robust and creative solutions.

Moreover, working with others can help to reduce stress and anxiety, which can contribute to creative blocks. By sharing the workload and ideas, you can feel less overwhelmed and more motivated to generate and refine new ideas.

Effective collaboration requires clear communication and mutual respect. It's essential to establish clear goals, roles, and expectations to ensure everyone is on the same page. Moreover, it's important to be open-minded and willing to listen to different perspectives and ideas.

Collaborating with others is an excellent strategy for overcoming creative blocks and generating new ideas. By working together, you can tap into new perspectives and knowledge, challenge each other's thinking, and develop more robust and creative solutions.

Try new techniques:

Trying new ideation techniques can help to break through creative blocks and generate fresh ideas. There are countless ideation techniques to choose from, ranging from traditional brainstorming and mind mapping to more unconventional methods like improv comedy and sensory exploration.

One example of a technique that can help generate new ideas is called "reverse brainstorming." In this technique, instead of generating ideas for how to solve a problem, you focus on generating ideas for how to worsen the problem. This can help to shift your perspective and identify potential solutions that you might not have thought of otherwise.

Another technique is "forced connections," where you try to find connections between seemingly unrelated concepts or ideas. For example, you might try to connect the concept of "fast food" with "environmental sustainability." This can help to stimulate new ideas and generate creative solutions.

By trying out different ideation techniques, you can discover which ones work best for you and your team and continue to experiment and refine your approach to ideation.

Set constraints:

Setting constraints is a technique that can help overcome creative blocks and generate more focused and innovative ideas. Constraints can come in various forms, such as limited resources, time constraints, specific customer needs, or industry regulations.

By setting constraints, ideators are forced to think outside the box and come up with unique solutions to the given problem. For example, a limited budget may lead to finding more affordable and efficient ways to produce a product, while a time constraint may require finding quicker ways to deliver the product or service to the customer.

Setting constraints can also help narrow down the focus and scope of ideation, making it easier to generate more specific and relevant ideas. This can be particularly useful in situations where there are too many possibilities and options, making it difficult to choose the most promising ones.

It is important to note that constraints should not be so limiting that they stifle creativity or prevent the exploration of new ideas altogether. It is essential to strike a balance between providing enough guidance and structure to encourage innovation while allowing for flexibility and exploration.

By using these tips, entrepreneurs can overcome creative blocks and continue to generate and refine new business ideas.

5.2 Dealing with idea overload

Idea overload can be overwhelming and make it difficult to focus on the most promising ideas. Here are some tips for dealing with idea overload:

Prioritize:

Prioritizing is an essential step in dealing with idea overload. When you have too many ideas, it's easy to get overwhelmed and not know where to start. Prioritizing helps you focus on the most important and promising ideas.
One way to prioritize is to use a scoring system. Assign a score to each idea based on criteria such as feasibility, profitability, and alignment with your values and goals. Then rank the ideas based on their scores.

Another way to prioritize is to use a decision matrix. Create a table with the ideas on one axis and criteria on the other. Assign weights to each criterion based on its importance. Then score each idea on each criterion and calculate a total score for each idea. This method can help you make more objective decisions.

It's also important to consider your available resources when prioritizing. Some ideas may require more time, money, or expertise than you have available. Prioritizing based on what you can realistically accomplish can help you avoid taking on too much at once and burning out.

Categorize:

When you have too many ideas, it can be helpful to categorize them into groups or themes. This helps to organize your thoughts and makes it easier to identify which ideas are related and which ones can be combined or discarded. For example, if you are generating ideas for a new product, you may categorize them by features, target market, or pricing strategy.

Categorizing your ideas can also help you to identify any gaps or areas where you may need to do more research or generate additional ideas. By looking at your categories as a whole, you can see if there are any themes that are underrepresented or if there are any areas where you may need to generate more ideas.

There are many ways to categorize your ideas, depending on your specific goals and the type of ideas you are generating. You may choose to use a simple list format, or you may prefer to use a visual tool such as a mind map or a diagram to organize your ideas into categories. Whatever method you choose, the goal is to create a system that works for you and helps you to manage your ideas effectively.

Validate:

When you have too many ideas, it can be difficult to decide which one(s) to pursue. One way to narrow down your options is to validate your ideas. This means testing them to see if they have potential for success in the marketplace.

Validation can take many forms, such as conducting market research, creating a prototype or MVP (minimum viable product), or getting feedback from potential customers or industry experts. The goal is to gather data and insights that can help you determine which ideas are worth pursuing and which ones may need to be discarded or put on hold.

One common approach to validation is to use the "lean startup" methodology, which emphasizes rapid experimentation and feedback to quickly iterate and improve upon an idea. This involves creating a basic prototype or MVP and testing it with a small group of users to gauge interest and identify areas for improvement.

Validation can also involve seeking out potential customers or industry experts and getting their feedback on your idea. This can be done through surveys, focus groups, or one-on-one interviews. By talking to your target market and gathering their input, you can better understand their needs and preferences, which can inform your product or service development.

The key to dealing with idea overload is to focus on quality over quantity. By validating your ideas and prioritizing those with the most potential, you can ensure that you're spending your time and resources on the ideas that are most likely to succeed.

Test:

Testing is an important step in dealing with idea overload. Once you have prioritized and categorized your ideas, it's time to test them to see which ones have the most potential. This involves creating prototypes or minimum viable products (MVPs) and testing them with your target market.

The goal of testing is to gather feedback and data that will help you refine and improve your ideas. This can include feedback on the product or service itself, as well as feedback on pricing, marketing, and other aspects of the business.

There are many different ways to test your ideas, depending on the nature of your business and your target market. Some common methods include:

- A/B testing: This involves creating two versions of a product or marketing campaign and testing them to see which performs better.
- User testing: This involves gathering feedback from users on a prototype or MVP.
- Surveys: Surveys can be used to gather feedback on product features, pricing, marketing messages, and other aspects of the business.
- Focus groups: Focus groups allow you to gather feedback from a group of people in a structured setting.
- Landing pages: Landing pages can be used to test interest in a product or service before it is fully developed.

By testing your ideas, you can identify the ones with the most potential and avoid wasting time and resources on ideas that are unlikely to succeed. Testing also allows you to make data-driven decisions about your business, which can increase your chances of success.

Refine:

Refining an idea is an iterative process that involves making improvements and adjustments based on feedback and testing. Once you have a prototype or a minimum viable product (MVP), you can gather feedback from users or customers to identify areas for improvement. This feedback can come from surveys, user testing sessions, or reviews, among other sources.

Once you have collected feedback, it is important to analyze it and identify patterns and common themes. Based on this analysis, you can identify specific areas that need improvement and develop a plan to make those changes. This could involve adjusting features or functionality, improving the user experience, or addressing any technical issues that have been identified.

After you have made the necessary changes, it is important to test your refined idea again to ensure that it is meeting the needs of your target market. This process of testing and refining should continue until you have a product or service that is ready to be launched or scaled.

Refining an idea is an essential part of the ideation process, as it allows you to make necessary adjustments and improvements that can ultimately lead to a successful product or service. By gathering feedback, analyzing it, and making informed changes, you can ensure that your idea is meeting the needs of your target market and is positioned for success.

Remember, it's important to stay focused on your goals and objectives, and avoid getting distracted by too many ideas. By using these strategies, you can effectively manage idea overload and develop the most promising ideas for your business.

By using these strategies, you can effectively manage idea overload and develop the most promising ideas for your business.

5.3 Managing team dynamics in ideation

Managing team dynamics in ideation is essential to ensure that everyone is contributing to the ideation process and the team is functioning effectively.

Here are some ways to manage team dynamics in ideation:

Establish clear roles and responsibilities:

Establishing clear roles and responsibilities is crucial in managing team dynamics during the ideation process. When team members are uncertain about their roles, they may struggle to contribute effectively, which can lead to frustration, resentment, and conflicts. Therefore, it's essential to define each team member's role, responsibilities, and expectations at the beginning of the project.

To establish clear roles and responsibilities, the team leader should first identify the specific tasks that need to be accomplished and then assign them to team members based on their skills, experience, and interests. Each team member should have a clear understanding of what they are responsible for and what is expected of them.

It's important to set up a communication plan that outlines how team members will communicate with each other, how often they will meet, and what channels they will use for communication. This plan can help ensure that everyone is on the same page and that there are no misunderstandings or communication breakdowns.

Regular check-ins and progress updates can also help ensure that everyone is on track and that any issues are addressed promptly. If any team members are struggling, the team leader can provide additional support or training to help them get up to speed.

By establishing clear roles and responsibilities and fostering open communication, team members can work together more effectively and create a positive and productive environment for ideation.

Foster a collaborative environment:

Fostering a collaborative environment is crucial in managing team dynamics during the ideation process. Collaboration encourages the sharing of ideas, improves communication, and helps to build trust among team members.

Here are some ways to foster a collaborative environment:

Encourage open communication:

Create an environment where team members can express their thoughts and ideas freely without fear of criticism or judgment. Encourage active listening and consider every idea, no matter how unconventional it may seem.

Build trust:

Trust is crucial in any collaborative environment. Trust allows team members to rely on one another and builds a foundation for collaboration. Encourage transparency, honesty, and openness in all communication.

Emphasize teamwork:

Reinforce the idea that the project's success is a team effort. Encourage team members to work together and emphasize the importance of collaboration.

Foster a culture of creativity:

Encourage creativity and experimentation among team members. Celebrate new ideas and encourage team members to think outside the box.

Provide opportunities for team building:

Create opportunities for team members to bond outside of work. This can include team outings, group projects, or team-building exercises.

By fostering a collaborative environment, team members are more likely to work together effectively, share ideas openly, and generate more innovative solutions.

Set clear expectations:

Setting clear expectations is important in managing team dynamics during ideation. This includes communicating the project's goals, timeline, budget, and other relevant information to team members. By setting clear expectations, team members have a better understanding of their role in the project and what is expected of them.

When setting expectations, it's important to make sure they are realistic and achievable. This helps to avoid misunderstandings or conflicts that may arise if expectations are not met. In addition, it's important to be open to feedback from team members and to adjust expectations as needed based on their input.

Clear expectations also help to hold team members accountable for their work. By setting specific goals and timelines, team members can track their progress and ensure that they are on track to meet their objectives. It also allows team leaders to identify any potential issues or delays and address them early on.

Setting clear expectations is an important part of managing team dynamics in ideation. It helps to create a more collaborative and productive environment, and ensures that everyone is on the same page when it comes to project goals and objectives.

Embrace diversity:

Embracing diversity is an important aspect of managing team dynamics in ideation. When team members come from different backgrounds, experiences, and perspectives, they bring unique ideas and insights to the table. By embracing diversity, teams can generate a wider range of ideas, identify potential blind spots, and come up with more creative solutions to problems.

To embrace diversity, it's important to create an environment where all team members feel comfortable sharing their ideas and perspectives, regardless of their background or experience. This can be achieved by setting ground rules for communication, encouraging active listening, and creating opportunities for open dialogue and discussion.

Team leaders can also encourage diversity by intentionally seeking out team members with different backgrounds and experiences. This can include recruiting from diverse talent pools, partnering with organizations that promote diversity, or actively seeking out individuals with different perspectives.

By embracing diversity and creating an inclusive team environment, teams can effectively manage team dynamics in ideation, foster creativity, and generate innovative ideas.

Address conflicts promptly:

In any team or group, conflicts may arise due to differences in opinions, ideas, or ways of working. These conflicts, if not addressed promptly, can escalate and negatively impact the team's dynamics and productivity. It is crucial to have a process in place for conflict resolution and to address conflicts promptly.

One way to address conflicts is to have an open and honest conversation with the parties involved, allowing each person to express their perspective and concerns. Encourage active listening and avoid blaming or attacking language. Instead, focus on understanding each other's perspectives and finding common ground.

Another way to address conflicts is to involve a neutral third party, such as a mediator or team leader, to facilitate the conversation and help find a resolution. This can be particularly helpful when emotions are high, and the parties involved are having difficulty communicating effectively.

It is also essential to establish a team culture that values diversity and encourages constructive feedback. By embracing diversity, the team can leverage different perspectives and approaches to solve problems and generate new ideas.

Addressing conflicts promptly and fostering a collaborative environment can help manage team dynamics in ideation and ensure that the team is working together effectively towards a common goal.

Celebrate successes:

Celebrating successes is an important aspect of managing team dynamics in ideation. Recognizing and celebrating individual and team achievements can help build morale and motivation, and can encourage team members to continue to work hard and innovate.

Celebrating successes can take many forms, from simple gestures like congratulatory messages or team lunches, to more elaborate events like company-wide celebrations or recognition programs. The key is to ensure that team members feel valued and appreciated for their contributions, and that their efforts are recognized and rewarded.

In addition to boosting morale and motivation, celebrating successes can also help reinforce the importance of the team's goals and objectives, and can help maintain momentum and focus. It can also help build a positive team culture that values collaboration, innovation, and continuous improvement.

By effectively managing team dynamics, you can ensure that your team is working collaboratively towards a common goal and producing high-quality, innovative ideas.

5.4 Balancing creativity with feasibility

Balancing creativity with feasibility is a critical aspect of ideation, as it ensures that the ideas generated are both innovative and practical. While it's important to come up with creative and out-of-the-box ideas, it's equally essential to evaluate their feasibility before pursuing them.

One way to balance creativity with feasibility is by applying design thinking principles, which involve understanding the users' needs, prototyping, and testing the ideas. This approach helps identify the most feasible ideas that also offer value to the users.

Another approach is to establish criteria for evaluating ideas, including factors such as cost, time, resources, and potential return on investment. By considering these criteria, teams can prioritize ideas that are both creative and feasible, and develop action plans that align with the available resources and budget.

It's essential to involve stakeholders and experts from various disciplines in the ideation process. This allows for a diverse range of perspectives, and helps ensure that the ideas generated are both innovative and practical.

Teams must be willing to iterate and refine their ideas based on feedback and testing. This process helps identify and address any feasibility concerns, while also continuing to build on the creativity and innovation of the idea.

VI. Ideation for Different Types of Businesses

In this section, we will explore how ideation can be applied to different types of businesses. Each business model has its unique challenges, opportunities, and constraints that influence the ideation process. We will examine how ideation can be used in various types of businesses, such as product-based businesses, service-based businesses, and online businesses. Additionally, we will explore how ideation can be applied to startups and established businesses, highlighting the differences in the ideation process for each.

6.1 Ideation for technology startups

Ideation for technology startups involves identifying and solving problems through the use of technology. In this context, ideation focuses on creating innovative solutions that disrupt existing markets or create entirely new ones.

Ideation for technology startups often involves brainstorming ideas that leverage emerging technologies, such as artificial intelligence, blockchain, or the internet of things. Startups in this field must consider factors such as market demand, user experience, scalability, and technical feasibility when generating and evaluating ideas.

One common approach to ideation for technology startups is the "lean startup" methodology, which emphasizes rapid experimentation and iteration to test and refine ideas. This approach involves creating minimum viable products (MVPs) to test assumptions and validate market demand before investing significant resources in product development.

Ideation for technology startups requires a blend of creative thinking, technical expertise, and business acumen to create solutions that are both innovative and viable in the marketplace.

6.2 Ideation for service-based businesses

Ideation for service-based businesses can be approached in a similar manner to product-based businesses, but with some key differences. Instead of focusing on physical products, the emphasis is on creating innovative services that meet the needs and wants of customers.

One approach to ideation for service-based businesses is to start by identifying customer pain points and areas where existing services may be lacking. This can be done through market research techniques such as surveys, focus groups, and interviews.

Once pain points are identified, brainstorm potential services that can solve these problems and add value to customers' lives. Service ideas can range from consulting and coaching services to professional services like accounting or legal advice, to home services like cleaning and landscaping.
It is also important to consider the user experience when developing service ideas. This includes factors such as ease of use, convenience, and accessibility. For example, a service that is easy to use and accessible through a mobile app may be more attractive to customers than one that requires a phone call or email to book.

Testing and validation are crucial steps in the ideation process for service-based businesses. This can involve creating prototypes or minimum viable products (MVPs) to test with customers, gathering feedback, and refining the service based on this feedback.

Ideation for service-based businesses requires a focus on customer needs, innovation, and user experience to create valuable and compelling services that stand out in a competitive market.

6.3 Ideation for social enterprises

social enterprises are businesses that aim to have a positive social or environmental impact while also generating revenue. When ideating for social enterprises, it's important to prioritize the social or environmental mission while also considering the feasibility of the business model.

One approach to ideation for social enterprises is to identify a social or environmental problem and brainstorm business solutions that address the problem while also generating revenue. For example, a social enterprise might aim to reduce food waste by creating a food delivery service that collects surplus food from restaurants and distributes it to people in need.

Another approach is to identify a particular community or group that is underserved and brainstorm business solutions that meet their needs. For example, a social enterprise might aim to provide affordable housing for low-income families in a particular city.

When ideating for social enterprises, it's also important to consider potential partnerships with non-profit organizations, government agencies, or other businesses that share the same social or environmental mission. These partnerships can provide access to resources and expertise that can help the social enterprise achieve its goals.

6.4 Ideation for corporate innovation

Ideation for corporate innovation involves generating and implementing new ideas within an established company. This type of ideation is often focused on improving existing products, services, or processes, or creating new ones, in order to stay competitive and meet the changing needs of customers.

One approach to ideation for corporate innovation is to establish a dedicated innovation team or department, which is tasked with exploring new ideas and developing strategies for implementation. This team can be made up of employees from various departments within the company, and may also involve external consultants or experts.

Another approach is to encourage innovation and ideation among all employees, through training programs, workshops, and other initiatives. This can help to foster a culture of innovation within the company, where employees are encouraged to think creatively and share their ideas.

When ideating for corporate innovation, it's important to consider factors such as market trends, customer needs, and potential competition.

Additionally, feasibility, cost-effectiveness, and alignment with the company's goals and values are also important considerations.

Once ideas have been generated, they can be evaluated using various techniques such as SWOT analysis, cost-benefit analysis, and risk assessment. After selecting the most promising ideas, the company can begin the prototyping and testing process before implementing the chosen innovation.

Ideation for corporate innovation requires a balance between creativity and practicality, and a willingness to take calculated risks in order to stay competitive in the market.

VII. Ideation for Personal Development

Ideation is not only limited to developing business ideas, but it can also be a powerful tool for personal development. The process of ideation can help individuals generate new and innovative ideas for personal growth and self-improvement. In this section, we will explore how ideation can be used for personal development and offer some tips and techniques for generating creative ideas that can help you achieve your personal goals.

7.1 Using ideation for career development

Ideation can be a valuable tool for career development, as it helps individuals generate new ideas for their professional growth and identify opportunities for advancement.

To start, individuals can brainstorm ideas for how they want to progress in their career, whether that means moving up in their current company or transitioning to a new industry. This can involve identifying their strengths and areas for improvement, researching potential job roles, and networking with professionals in their desired field.

Once they have a list of potential career paths or goals, individuals can evaluate each idea by conducting research on the industry, job responsibilities, required skills and qualifications, and potential salary and benefits. They can also seek advice from mentors or career coaches to gain further insights and guidance.

Individuals can develop action plans for pursuing their chosen career paths, which may include acquiring new skills or certifications, updating their resume and online presence, and networking with professionals in their desired field. By using ideation as a tool for career development, individuals can explore new possibilities and take intentional steps towards achieving their professional goals.

7.2 Using ideation for personal growth

Using ideation techniques can be very helpful for personal growth, as it allows individuals to explore their interests, passions, and potential opportunities for self-improvement.

Here are some ways in which ideation can be used for personal growth:

Brainstorming:

Brainstorming can be used to generate a list of personal goals or aspirations, whether it's learning a new skill, trying a new hobby, or pursuing a new career path.

Mind mapping:

Mind mapping can help individuals visualize their personal growth goals and the steps needed to achieve them. It can also help identify potential roadblocks or challenges that may need to be addressed.

SWOT analysis:

A SWOT analysis can be used to assess an individual's strengths, weaknesses, opportunities, and threats in relation to their personal growth goals. This can help them identify areas where they need to focus their efforts and develop a plan to overcome obstacles.

Feedback and evaluation:

Just as in a business setting, feedback and evaluation can be useful in personal growth as well. Seeking feedback from others, tracking progress towards personal goals, and evaluating successes and failures can help individuals identify areas where they need to improve and adjust their approach.

Using ideation techniques for personal growth can help individuals explore their potential, set meaningful goals, and develop a plan to achieve them.

7.3 Using ideation for lifelong learning

Ideation can be a powerful tool for lifelong learning, as it allows individuals to generate new ideas and explore new concepts.

Here are some ways that ideation can be used for lifelong learning:

Brainstorming new learning topics:

Use ideation techniques such as mind mapping or brainstorming to generate ideas for new topics to learn about. This can help to identify areas of interest and create a roadmap for lifelong learning.

Designing personal learning projects:

Use ideation to design personal learning projects that align with individual goals and interests. This can involve setting learning objectives, identifying resources and materials, and developing a plan for implementation.

Exploring new learning modalities:

Use ideation to explore new learning modalities, such as online courses, podcasts, or workshops. This can help to identify new ways to engage with material and expand the range of learning opportunities available.

Developing learning communities:

Use ideation to develop learning communities, such as book clubs or study groups, that can support ongoing learning and provide opportunities for collaboration and feedback.

Ideation can be a valuable tool for those interested in lifelong learning, providing a structured approach to exploring new ideas and identifying opportunities for growth and development.

7.4 Using ideation for creative hobbies

Painting, writing, music, or any other form of art, ideation can help generate new ideas and push creative boundaries.

Here are some ways to use ideation for creative hobbies:

- Brainstorming: Set aside time to brainstorm new ideas for your creative hobby. Write down every idea that comes to mind, even if it seems silly or impractical. The goal is to generate a large quantity of ideas, which can then be refined and developed into something more concrete.

- Mind Mapping: Use mind mapping to visualize your ideas and how they relate to each other. Start with a central idea, such as a theme or concept, and then branch out to related ideas. This can help you see connections between different ideas and develop a more cohesive creative project.

- Constraints: Set constraints or limitations for your creative project to challenge yourself and generate new ideas. For example, try writing a story using only 100 words or creating a painting using only three colors.

- Feedback: Share your work with others and ask for feedback. This can help you identify areas for improvement and generate new ideas for your next project.

- Experimentation: Try new techniques or materials to push your creative boundaries and generate new ideas. Don't be afraid to take risks and try something new.

The goal of using ideation for creative hobbies is not necessarily to create a masterpiece, but to explore new ideas and push creative boundaries. Have fun and enjoy the process!

VIII. Conclusion

Throughout this book, we have explored the process of ideation and how it can be applied to various aspects of life, from entrepreneurship to personal development. We have discussed various techniques and methods for generating and refining ideas, as well as strategies for managing team dynamics and overcoming common challenges.

Ideation is a powerful tool that can help individuals and organizations to innovate, grow, and achieve their goals. By engaging in a structured process of ideation, individuals can develop the skills and mindset necessary for success in today's rapidly changing world.

As we conclude this book, it is our hope that you have gained a deeper understanding of ideation and its potential for creating positive change in your life and the world around you. We encourage you to continue exploring and experimenting with ideation, and to never stop learning, growing, and challenging yourself to think creatively and innovatively.

8.1 Key takeaways from the book

here are some key takeaways from the book:

- Ideation is the process of generating, developing, and refining new ideas.

- The ideation process is crucial for entrepreneurs, innovators, and individuals looking to improve their personal and professional lives.

- Effective ideation requires a combination of creativity, research, and practicality.

- The ideation process can be broken down into several stages, including problem identification, idea generation, feedback, refinement, and implementation.

- Techniques such as brainstorming, mind mapping, and SCAMPER can be used to generate new ideas.

- Validating and testing ideas with market research and feedback from potential customers is important for ensuring their viability.

- Collaborating with others can help overcome creative blocks and enhance the quality of ideas.

- Managing team dynamics is crucial for successful ideation in group settings.

- Balancing creativity with feasibility is key for developing sustainable and profitable ideas.

- The ideation process can be applied to a range of contexts, including technology startups, service-based businesses, social enterprises, and personal development.

By following the strategies and techniques outlined in this book, readers can improve their ability to generate, develop, and implement innovative ideas in a variety of settings.

8.2 Practical tips for ideation success

Here are some practical tips for ideation success:

Embrace curiosity:

Curiosity is key to ideation. Explore different areas, ask questions, and don't be afraid to challenge assumptions.

Use diverse ideation methods:

Experiment with a range of ideation methods to find what works best for you and your team. Combining different methods can lead to more innovative and diverse ideas.

Keep an open mind:

Be open to feedback and new ideas, even if they challenge your assumptions. Encourage others to share their thoughts and build on them.

Test and iterate:

Test your ideas early and often, and be willing to make changes and iterate based on feedback. This helps ensure that your ideas are viable and can be implemented successfully.

Collaborate effectively:

Work with others in a collaborative and respectful way. Clearly define roles and responsibilities, communicate openly, and address conflicts promptly.

Prioritize and focus:

Focus on the most promising ideas and prioritize them based on feasibility, impact, and other relevant criteria. This helps ensure that you are allocating resources effectively and achieving your goals.

Stay flexible: Stay flexible and adaptable as you move through the ideation process. Be prepared to adjust your approach as new information and feedback emerge.

By following these practical tips, you can increase your chances of ideation success and bring your ideas to life.

8.3 The future of ideation in entrepreneurship

The future of ideation in entrepreneurship looks bright, with new tools and technologies emerging that make it easier than ever to generate and refine ideas. As the global business landscape continues to evolve, entrepreneurs will need to stay nimble and adaptive in their approach to ideation, staying attuned to emerging trends and changing consumer demands.

Some of the key trends shaping the future of ideation in entrepreneurship include:

Embracing innovation:

With advances in AI, machine learning, and other emerging technologies, entrepreneurs will need to be open to new ways of thinking about ideation. They'll need to be willing to experiment with new tools and techniques to stay ahead of the curve.

Collaborating across borders:

As the world becomes increasingly interconnected, entrepreneurs will need to be adept at collaborating with others from diverse cultural backgrounds. They'll need to be able to communicate effectively across borders and work with teams located in different parts of the world.

Focusing on sustainability:

With increasing concerns around climate change and environmental sustainability, entrepreneurs will need to be mindful of the impact their ideas have on the planet. They'll need to be able to integrate sustainability into their ideation process and prioritize eco-friendly solutions.

Embracing diversity and inclusion:

As the world becomes more diverse, entrepreneurs will need to be able to embrace diversity and inclusion in their ideation process. They'll need to be able to work with people from diverse backgrounds and perspectives, and create solutions that meet the needs of a diverse range of consumers.

The future of ideation in entrepreneurship is exciting and full of potential. By staying attuned to emerging trends and embracing new tools and techniques, entrepreneurs can continue to innovate and create impactful solutions that make a difference in the world.

8.4 Final thoughts on ideation and innovation

In conclusion, ideation is a crucial component of innovation and entrepreneurship. Generating and refining ideas is a continuous process that requires creativity, collaboration, and practicality. Through the different stages of ideation, entrepreneurs can develop a clear understanding of their target audience, their value proposition, and the feasibility of their ideas.

Some key takeaways from this book include the importance of understanding the problem before proposing a solution, the value of collaboration and diverse perspectives in ideation, and the significance of testing and validating ideas.

To achieve success in ideation, it is important to set clear goals, embrace ambiguity and failure, and create an environment that fosters creativity and innovation.

Looking to the future, the field of ideation is constantly evolving with the emergence of new technologies and changing consumer needs. Entrepreneurs must continue to adapt and innovate to stay ahead of the curve.

Ideation is an essential skill for any entrepreneur looking to create a successful and sustainable business. By following the principles and strategies outlined in this book, entrepreneurs can develop and refine their ideas, overcome challenges, and achieve their goals.

Innovation is the driving force behind progress and growth in business and society. Ideation, the process of generating and developing new ideas, is essential for innovation to occur. This book has explored the various aspects of ideation, from the ideation process itself to the challenges that individuals and teams face when trying to come up with new ideas.

One key takeaway from this book is that ideation is not just a one-time event, but rather a continuous process that requires ongoing effort and attention. To be successful in ideation, individuals and teams must foster a creative environment, use various ideation techniques, and be open to feedback and iteration. By following these principles, individuals and teams can generate and refine ideas that have the potential to change the world.

Another key takeaway is that ideation is not limited to any specific industry or type of business. Whether you are a technology startup, a service-based business, a social enterprise, or a corporate innovator, ideation can play a crucial role in your success. The strategies and techniques outlined in this book can be applied to a wide range of businesses and industries, making ideation an essential skill for anyone looking to succeed in today's fast-paced and competitive business environment.

One practical tip for ideation success is to focus on solving real-world problems. By identifying problems that people face and developing innovative solutions to these problems, individuals and teams can create products and services that have real value in the marketplace. This approach not only increases the likelihood of success but also provides a sense of purpose and fulfillment for those involved in the ideation process.

Another practical tip is to embrace diversity and foster a collaborative environment. By bringing together individuals with different backgrounds, skills, and perspectives, teams can generate ideas that are more innovative and impactful than those generated by homogeneous teams. By creating a culture of collaboration and openness to new ideas, individuals and teams can overcome creative blocks and generate ideas that have the potential to transform their businesses and industries.

The role of ideation in entrepreneurship is likely to become even more critical. With technological advancements and increasing competition, businesses must continue to innovate and evolve to remain relevant and competitive. Ideation provides a pathway for individuals and teams to generate new ideas and create value for their customers and stakeholders.

Ideation is an essential component of innovation and growth in business and society. By embracing the ideation process, individuals and teams can generate and refine ideas that have the potential to change the world. Whether you are an entrepreneur, a business owner, or simply someone looking to develop new skills, the strategies and techniques outlined in this book can help you succeed in today's fast-paced and ever-changing business environment.